Original title:
The Paradise of Palms

Copyright © 2025 Creative Arts Management OÜ
All rights reserved.

Author: Arabella Whitmore
ISBN HARDBACK: 978-1-80581-480-1
ISBN PAPERBACK: 978-1-80581-007-0
ISBN EBOOK: 978-1-80581-480-1

Stories Told by the Leaves

Whispering tales from the breeze,
Leaves gossip like old-time tease.
A coconut fell with a thud,
And laughed as it rolled in the mud.

Parrots croon in colorful suits,
Mimicking oddball local toots.
The sun plays hide-and-seek with the sky,
While lizards dance as they stroll by.

A Canvas of Tropical Tides

Brush strokes of green, quite absurd,
Seagulls argue, have you heard?
They squabble over a missing fry,
While the fish roll their eyes nearby.

Sandy toes and some suntan oils,
Children giggle, with innocent spoils.
Sandcastle knights keep watch from their posts,
While crabs plot on what they'd like most.

Radiant Refuge of Palm Shadows

In the shade where tall palms sway,
Sunburned tourists softly lay.
With floppy hats on floors of sand,
Dreaming about a cool drink in hand.

The breeze tickles sunburned cheeks,
While silly pelicans strike goofy peaks.
They pose for photos, look so grand,
Until they drop fish with their hand.

Where Sunshine Meets Silhouettes

Underneath the radiant glare,
Laughter bubbles up in the air.
A sunhat flies, caught by a breeze,
Followed by kids in a game of tease.

With every sunset's golden hue,
Stars peek out for a grand debut.
While people dance like wannabe pros,
We all laugh at the way that it goes.

Island Echoes of Serenity

In the shade of a leafy friend,
Lizards dance and the day won't end.
Coconuts laugh, they wiggle and sway,
While the sun sets the sky into play.

Hammocks swing with a sleepy creak,
Even seagulls stop to sneak.
Locals sip juice from a curvy straw,
As the tides clap their watery paw.

Tropical Tapestry of Relaxation

Pineapples wear crowns that just won't quit,
While flamingos strut in a stylish split.
When the breeze sings a breezy tune,
The bananas hum to the waxing moon.

Sandy toes wiggle in cozy bliss,
As crabs join in with a scuttling kiss.
The sun giggles as it twirls around,
On this vibrant playground, joy is found.

A Sanctuary of Silhouettes

Palm trees whisper secrets so tall,
While coconuts cater to our call.
Turtles wear shades, looking quite cool,
Trying hard to break the swimming pool rule.

Fish parade in colors so bright,
Making every splash a hilarious sight.
As the evening draws near, they play tag,
While the moon gets comfy in its little rag.

Embracing the Echoes of the Tropics

Boys chase crabs on the sunlit shores,
While giggles mingle with ocean roars.
A parrot cracks jokes from a high, green throne,
Saying, 'Don't worry, you're never alone!'

A picnic unfolds under the bright sun,
Sandwiches wobble, who'll have the most fun?
Jellyfish wiggle in a waltz so strange,
In this wild circus, nothing feels deranged.

Nature's Canopy Above Us

Leaves that sway and dance so free,
A monkey swings like it's on tea.
Jokes are whispered by the breeze,
While birds mimic our sneezes.

Laughter echoes in the shade,
Where sunshine and jokes are played.
Each palm tree tells a funny tale,
Of squirrels sneaking snacks without fail.

The Whispers of an Emerald Haven

Bamboo tickles with a cheeky grin,
An iguana smirks as we begin.
Frogs croak tunes that would charm a toad,
While lizards strut down their own road.

Butterflies flutter with a wink,
As they sip nectar, and pause to think.
Who knew flowers could gossip so loud,
As bees buzz by in a buzzing crowd?

Bordering the Horizon: A Tropical Escape

Sandy toes and a sunburned nose,
Sandcastles wobble like clumsy bros.
Waves giggle at the silly shore,
As crabs scuttle in a playful chore.

Seagulls squawk like they own the place,
Diving down for a fishy embrace.
While coconuts drop with a thud,
Causing beachgoers to jump in the mud.

Cradled in Cardamom and Palm Fronds

Underneath the fronds so grand,
We sip drinks with a playful hand.
A parrot squawks, "Don't spill your tea!"
As we laugh 'til we're light as a bee.

Fragrant spice fills up the air,
While we chase each other without a care.
Cardamom giggles in our cups,
As we join in with the tropical pups.

Reveries in Sun-kissed Hues

In a land where the coconuts sigh,
Lemons wiggle and giggle nearby.
The sun wears shades, that's quite a sight,
While flamingos dance with pure delight.

A parrot tells jokes, quite absurd,
While a lazy cat just naps and purrs.
The waves keep laughing, oh what a tease,
As we sip our drinks with zest and ease.

Beneath the Starry Palms

Under the stars, the coconuts sway,
While crabs perform in a clumsy ballet.
The fish join in with a splashy cheer,
As dolphins giggle, 'Come dance over here!'

With twinkling lights strung high in the trees,
The raccoons plot to steal all the cheese.
A night filled with laughter, oh so grand,
As the moon picks its favorite band.

The Calm After the Breeze

When gentle whispers brush the shore,
Seashells gossip, beg for more.
A crab scuttles, wearing a hat,
While a seagull squawks, 'Is that a mat?'

The sun takes a bow, it's time to rest,
As turtles join in, they're quite the jest.
With giggles and winks, the evening glows,
As the breeze teases our sunburnt toes.

Tranquil Shades of Green

In the jungle, cheeky monkeys swing,
As colorful parrots begin to sing.
The frogs join in, they've got the beat,
While sloths just hang, oh, what a feat!

With each rustle, a squirrel will dart,
Trading nuts for jokes, it's quite the art.
A dance-off ensues among the trees,
As laughter echoes with such great ease.

Where Paradise Kisses the Earth

Under palm leaves, a squirrel sneaks,
Nabbing coconuts, playing hide and seek.
Laughter echoes, the sun shines bright,
While crabs do the cha-cha in sheer delight.

Fronds dance gently in the warm sea breeze,
As tourists trip and stumble with unease.
Flip-flops flying, oh what a sight,
A conga line starts, with pure delight!

Coconuts giggle, tickling the ground,
As seagulls gossip in shrill, silly sounds.
The sun winks knowingly, casting its glow,
In this wacky wonder where good vibes flow.

With ice cream melting, it's sticky and sweet,
Even the crabs join in, dancing on feet.
Barefoot in bliss, all cares disappear,
In this dreamy place where joy is near.

Dreams Unfurled Under the Canopy

Beneath the fronds, a hammock swings,
While monkeys invent odd little things.
They juggle coconuts, cheerfully bold,
The crowd roars with laughter, it's pure gold!

Bananas wear sunglasses, looking quite cool,
As parrots discuss who's the biggest fool.
Under the sun, all chatter takes flight,
With fish playing poker, what a delight!

A crab with a hat, so proud and so grand,
Claims he's the king of this sandy land.
With each silly scuttle, he claims his throne,
While seagulls critique him in mocking tone.

Countless moments wrapped in sheer glee,
With laughter that flows, wild and free.
So here in the shade, let joy unfurl,
In this quirky place, laughter spins and twirls.

Sun-Kissed Canopies

Beneath the broad and waving fronds,
A coconut fell—it's toast, it's blond!
Parrots chatter jokes and squawk,
While sunbathers dance around to rock.

Sipping drinks with umbrellas so neat,
We laugh at our sandy, sticky feet.
The sun burns bright, but don't we glow,
With laughter as light as a palm tree's flow.

Beneath the Fronds of Tranquility

In the shade, we stretch and snooze,
A gentle breeze shakes off our blues.
A crab scuttles by with a look so sly,
We wonder if he's headed to a shrimp fry.

The sun slips down, what a sight!
A squirrel steals a snack, oh what a fright!
We giggle and point, 'That's quite the thief!'
With shells to collect, we find our relief.

A Symphony of Rustling Palms

As the wind plays a tune through the trees,
We find our rhythm, do the palm tree squeeze!
A dance-off begins with a tiny lizard,
Who moves like he's got a hidden wizard!

The leaves clap along, keeping us on beat,
While crabs join in with their shuffling feet.
A round of applause for the vibrant scene,
In a tropical world that feels so serene.

Sunset's Embrace on Sandy Shores

The sun slides low, a golden disc,
We toast with drinks that we couldn't risk.
With colors that paint the sky so bright,
We laugh and joke at the sight of night.

As shadows stretch and laughter swells,
We collect our shells like little spells.
The tide whispers secrets to the shore,
And we dance, carefree, forevermore.

Tropical Serenade

In a land where pineapples dance,
Coconuts sing in a goofy prance.
Monkeys on branches, making a fuss,
Tickling the breeze as they catch the bus.

Sandals are flopping, flip-flops are loud,
Sipping on coconut milk, feeling proud.
Sunburns are forming on noses that glow,
Everyone laughs, it's the tropical show.

Beach balls are bouncing, no chance to fall,
While seagulls squawk out their own funny call.
Fruits wearing hats and sunglasses so bright,
It's a party, oh what a silly sight!

Whispering Leaves in the Breeze

Leaves gossip softly, oh what a tale,
Of picnics gone wrong, where sandwiches fail.
The fruits in the garden wear hats made of sun,
They giggle away, having so much fun.

A parrot is squawking, he's got jokes to share,
About a crab who forgot, and walked down the square.
Tropical fish in a pool, trying to dive,
They flop and they flounder, feel so alive!

With laughter and chatter up in the trees,
Even the lizards are dancing with ease.
Tickled by breezes, all fauna in sway,
A mirthful commotion throughout the whole day.

Oasis Dreams Under a Starry Sky

Stars are winking, making eyes at the night,
While cacti are plotting to start a food fight.
With mirages of burgers and fries on a plate,
The critters all laugh while they wait for their fate.

In an oasis, where humor flows fast,
Frogs wearing sunglasses are hopping at last.
A lazy iguana just snores through the show,
While palm fronds wave, "Come join, let's go!"

The moon has a grin, it hangs low and round,
Telling stories of clowns with no sense of sound.
In dreams made of giggles, take flight like a kite,
In this whimsical realm, the laughter feels right.

Palm Shadows at Dusk

As shadows grow long from the tall palm trees,
The crabs on the beach dance with shameless ease.
Underneath the glow of a sunset so grand,
Everyone joins in, lending a helping hand.

A chef with a flair in a bright floral shirt,
Serves up some snacks, like a true tasty expert.
With laughter erupting from all sides around,
Even the waves seem to giggle and bound.

The night wears a blanket of twinkling delight,
While fireflies flicker, with whimsy ignited.
As the palms sway gently, a night full of cheer,
Here's a toast to fun, with loved ones near!

Horizon's Edge Adorned with Green

Coconuts wobble on their high throne,
Waiting for squirrels with nuts of their own.
Seagulls squawk in a silly parade,
As I stumble in flip-flops, quite underpaid.

Palms dance around in a playful jig,
Their leaves whisper secrets, they're all a bit big.
Even the sun seems to chuckle and glow,
While I trip on my towel, oh how it does show!

Savoring Silence Under Tropical Canopies

Under these leaves, the world calms down,
Chill out, little lizard, don't wear that frown.
In this leafy retreat, I sip coconut juice,
While a mosquito thinks my arm is a moose.

Laughter of waves, they tickle my ears,
I argue with crabs, but they're full of cheers.
The breeze plays a tune, but it's slightly off-key,
As I nap on the sand, dreaming of me.

Luminescent Evenings in Verdant Halls

As the sun dips low, the fireflies arrive,
Twinkling like disco balls, looking so alive.
I attempt to catch one; oh what a sight!
End up swatting at shadows, not quite right.

With laughter and chips, the night stretches on,
Chickens are dancing, and a palm frond has won.
Even the stars giggle, shining so bright,
In this tangled jungle of delight and light.

Reflections in the Palm's Veil

Mirrors of water reflect my wild hair,
I check with a grin, do I have a flare?
Palm fronds wave gently, as if to agree,
That my dance moves are clearly not for a spree.

Waves bop along, they giggle and cheer,
"Keep going!" they holler, "Don't you dare fear!"
But my best moves are saved for a beach bonfire,
Falling in the sand, the only thing to inspire!

Chasing Reflections in Golden Light

In the mirror of the waves,
I see a crab doing the cha-cha,
stepping sideways, oh so sly,
who knew a shell could dance so high?

A gull steals fries from my plate,
I chase it down, but it's too late,
digging through sand with all my might,
who knew carbs could take flight at night?

The sunbeams tickle my toes,
while a breeze throws a playful pose,
a hat flies off, I give a chase,
but it lands on a dog's happy face!

Bikini-clad, I'm on a spree,
whirling like a wind-up bee,
the waves clap back with a splash,
I tumble, oh what a belly crash!

Beneath a Canopy of Eternal Summer

Tanning lotion in my eye,
I squint at clouds drifting by,
did I just see a rubber duck?
Or am I out of luck, out of luck?

A squirrel steals my breakfast toast,
while I'm left to whine and boast,
in my hammock, dreaming of snacks,
finding squirrels are crafty hacks!

Palm branches tickle the air,
a dance-off with sunshine's flair,
who knew shadows could groove so fast?
The palm trees know how to have a blast!

With a coconut drink in hand,
I'm the king of this sandy land,
only to find my straw's too short,
now it's a battle, what a sport!

Trails of Swaying Serenity

Walking on the beach, oh what a sight,
seagulls argue, it's quite a fight,
who's got the best shell in town?
It's a beauty pageant, no one frowns!

A kid builds castles made of sand,
while I'm stuck with the sun's hot brand,
"Watch out!" I hear, but it's too late,
a wave arrives, sealing my fate!

Shadows dance like they're in a play,
with my flip-flops leading the way,
they skip and hop, how very bold,
"Hey! Don't you know I'm not that old?"

Laughter spills with every tide,
a frisbee swoops on a wild ride,
missing hands, and then a face,
now we're all in a laughing race!

Moments Captured in Whispering Palms

Click! My camera captures the sound,
while a lizard strikes a silly pose,
"Cheese!" I shout, it runs away,
but I swear it winked, what a day!

Under palm fronds, lovebirds coo,
issues arise, like what to chew,
"Let's share," I suggest with glee,
but one bites back, now I can't see!

The sunset draws a canvas bright,
while I juggle my drink with delight,
who knew a straw could cause such fuss?
It's a slippery slope; please don't rush!

Sipping ice tea, I hear a laugh,
a crab joins in for the photograph,
a moment perfect, a giggle spree,
regretting the time it chased me, whee!

Skylines Wrapped in Green

High rises peek through leaves,
As squirrels plot their heists.
The pigeons make their moves,
In this city of mischief and feasts.

Bamboo shoots poke at the clouds,
While the sun laughs with glee.
Birds trade gossip like currency,
In a feathered jamboree.

Coconuts roll like bowling balls,
As laughter echoes around.
Even trees waggle their boughs,
In this nifty, verdant playground.

The horizon stretches wide,
With giggles and chortles galore.
Who knew green could be so bright,
In this lovely leafy store?

Tides of Time Beneath the Palms

The waves tickle tiny toes,
While seagulls steal your fries.
Time drips like melting ice,
Underneath those swaying skies.

Crabs throw a beachside dance,
With crabby little kicks.
A picnic lunch gone awry,
Turns into a game of tricks!

Sunset pours its mango glow,
As shadows stretch and yawn.
The breeze tells tales of days,
When silliness was born at dawn.

Footprints trip upon the sand,
As the tide pulls away.
With grins like the full moon bright,
Who knew fun was here to stay?

The Dance of Sunlight and Shade

Sunlight winks through the leaves,
As beams break into plays.
The grass whispers secrets low,
In a symphony of rays.

Lizards practice yoga moves,
On a path so winding.
There's a shade that hides a dance,
In a game of quick and blinding.

Bouncing balls of laughter roll,
Through a jungle of delight.
Each step taps on hidden beats,
As dusk puts on its night.

The stars peek shyly through trees,
In a twinkling, teasing show.
Who knew the night could giggle?
In the haven of sun's hello?

Where Dreams Glisten in Gold

Beneath bright blooms of yellow,
The world spins with a grin.
Ideas bounce like bumblebees,
In a rhythm that draws them in.

Pineapple hats are all the rage,
On this whimsical shore.
With dreams that shimmer and shine,
Who could ask for more?

Hammocks swing with silly tales,
As laughter drifts on by.
Each sloth wears a silly face,
Under that cotton candy sky.

Goals are set like beachside shells,
Bright treasures of the day.
In every grain of sand, we find,
A giggle tucked away.

Echoes of Love in Whispering Leaves

In the shade, the lovers meet,
With soft giggles that dance and greet.
A parrot squawks, it steals the show,
Love's hilarity in every blow.

They swap sweet tales, oh what a jest,
While the breeze gives the branches a test.
A mischief maker, the wind plays tricks,
Sending hats flying, oh what a mix!

Underneath, the ground is warm,
Tickling toes, a cheeky charm.
They laugh at ants in a parade,
As they join in, a tiny brigade.

With each rustle, the leaves confide,
Secrets of love, with humor wide.
In this laughter, hearts take flight,
Echoes of love dance through the night.

The Dreamer's Sanctuary

In a hammock, dreams unfold,
Where sloths move slow, but tales are bold.
A coconut drops with a clunk on the head,
'Just a reminder,' the dreamers said.

Stars wink down with silly grins,
As crickets toss in their violin spins.
A breeze whispers tales of sweet delight,
Where laughter spreads like the warm moonlight.

With fireflies winking, a dance begins,
Chasing shadows, where the fun never thins.
A twirl, a spin, and a jump in the air,
Dreamers find magic, without a care.

In this sanctuary, joy holds sway,
As whimsy and wonder come out to play.
Each fluttering leaf, each tittering sound,
Turns ordinary nights into bliss profound.

Between Sunlight and Shadows

Sunbeams poke through leaves so green,
Causing smiles where laughter's seen.
Elvis, the squirrel, struts with flair,
Wiggling his tail, without a care.

In shadows, giggles softly creep,
While turtles bask in dreams so deep.
A moment of calm, then a race begins,
With squeaks and beeps, oh what silly spins!

Laughter ripples as water flows,
Droplets leap, in bubbly shows.
The sun and shade in a playful dance,
Embrace the folly, give joy a chance.

So as the day melts into night,
Sunlight and shadows concoct delight.
Between their grip, happiness lives,
With laughter woven, the heart forgives.

A Celebration among the Palms

Beneath the palms, a feast laid wide,
With fruits galore and laughter inside.
A monkey swings, steals a banana,
Yelling, 'Fresh fruit, what a banter!'

Folks join in, they dance with glee,
Imitating squirrels, oh so free.
The conga line curls 'round a trunk,
With giggles and wiggles, oh what funk!

A picnic spread, where sandwiches fly,
Kites catch the wind, soaring high.
In the mix, a crab moonwalks the sand,
Leading the charge, a dance unplanned!

As twilight descends, the stars align,
Glowing bright, like sipping wine.
Here laughter reigns, under palm's embrace,
A celebration blooms, with joy and grace.

Vibrance of Life in Greenery's Grip

In a hammock, I do sway,
Bouncing gently, come what may.
A squirrel steals my snack with glee,
I chase him off—he laughs at me.

Bright red flowers dance and prance,
While bees take part in their romance.
A lizard grins upon a rock,
He's got moves that really shock!

The sun peeks through with golden beams,
As I plot my scheming dreams.
With every sip of coconut milk,
I feel more smooth, like silk in silk!

I spot my friend, a parrot bold,
Whose gossip always makes me scold.
Yet all around, such joy I find,
In this green world, so free and blind.

Connection to Earth and Sky

Clouds float by like fluffy sheep,
While ants march on, not missing a beat.
I wave at birds, who think I'm mad,
They squawk and laugh—my face is sad.

The grass tickles my wiggly toes,
It whispers secrets—who really knows?
A butterfly flutters, bold and brief,
While I just sit, in absolute grief!

The trees are chatting, oh so spry,
While I sip juice, just saying 'Hi!'
A breeze gives my hair a wild toss,
I pretend I'm the boss of the floss!

With roots deep down in the earth so snug,
I snicker at clouds, but then feel a tug.
Maybe I should dance and sway—
A funny fool at the end of the day!

Harmonies of Wind and Leaf

The wind sings songs to each green leaf,
While I strut by in a state of belief.
An iguana lounges, thinking it's cool,
While I look on, trying to act like a fool!

A monkey swings with effortless charm,
I wave cautiously, avoiding alarm.
A bashful breeze teases my sleeve,
I make a joke; the tree starts to heave!

Sunset hues splash the sky—so sweet,
As I trip over roots, tumbling feet.
The laughter of nature echoes all around,
In silly moments, we're truly found!

So here's to the laughter, the giggles we share,
With each rustling leaf, no room for despair.
I'm crowned by this crown of cheeky delight,
In nature's embrace, I'm dancing tonight!

The Call of the Tropical Breeze

In the jungle, the breezes play,
I hold my hat—let it not fly away!
A toucan caws, sharing the news,
'Watch your drink; the parrots may snooze!'

The sun beams down, a cheerful tease,
While I'm fanned by a mischievous breeze.
Palms sway gently, laughing out loud,
At me, the clumsy, an awkward cloud!

Each gust a whisper of joyful cheer,
Tickling cheeks and bringing good cheer.
Floating jokes from leaf to leaf,
While nature's mockery brings relief!

So here I stand, amid the fun,
Chasing colors, and feeling the sun.
In every moment, let laughter seize,
In this wild banquet of the tropical breeze!

Cascades of Leaves and Light

In a jungle gym of green,
Leaves leap like frogs unseen.
Sunlight does the hula dance,
While shadows wobble, caught in trance.

Monkeys with a curious gaze,
Swinging through the leafy maze.
Bananas fly and laughter peels,
Nature's big top, oh what reels!

Fronds flutter like they've gone wild,
Making every breeze beguiled.
Chasing bugs like they're the stars,
Giggles bubble up from jars.

Sipping nectar, bugs declare,
"Life's a party, come take care!"
In this wacky leafy spree,
I'm the main act—can't you see?

Retreat of Whispering Palms

Tall dancers swaying in a row,
Hands raised high, they steal the show.
Whispers of wind, a playful tease,
Who knew shrubs had such expertise?

One palm grumbles, "I'm too green,"
While others giggle, "What a scene!"
With trunks like legs in a limbo game,
They shimmy, twist—oh, what a fame!

Coconuts roll, a clumsy crowd,
As fronds erupt in giggles loud.
"Dare to dance!" the breeze jolts forth,
And palms respond with endless mirth.

In this crisp retreat, it's clear,
Life's a jest from front to rear.
So come unwind beneath the shade,
Join the laughter that won't fade!

An Eden Enclosed in Fronds

Amidst the greens where jokes do sprout,
Funny faces hide, no doubt.
Squirrels giggle in the trees,
Making mischief with the breeze.

The flowers wear their brightest hue,
Each one trying to outdo,
"Look at me!" they seem to yell,
"I'm the best! Come, ring my bell!"

Sunlight tickles every leaf,
Inviting laughter, disbelief.
Garden gnomes are on the prowl,
Raising eyebrows with a howl.

In this realm where whimsy thrives,
Nature tells the funniest lives.
So grab a seat, and take a look,
In frondy halls where laughter's hooked!

Nature's Embrace in Leafy Beginnings

Welcome to the leafy fair,
Where laughter skitters everywhere.
A toucan snaps a joke in flight,
While ferns giggle with delight.

A hedgehog in a leaf-made hat,
Winks at rabbits, "What's up, fat?"
In this embrace, the fun unfolds,
Nature's stories never get old.

Daisies sport their happy face,
Joking that they're in the race!
Bees buzz by with playful flair,
Stealing nectar, unaware.

As twilight wraps its arms around,
Laughter lingers; joy is found.
In every frond, a quip to share,
Join the dance—don't you dare!

A World Woven in Green

In a jungle of joy, oh what a scene,
Where squirrels wear hats and dance like a queen.
Lemons fall softly, no need to slice,
They bounce like rubber, oh isn't that nice?

Chorus of frogs belting tunes on their way,
While the parrots chatter, they just like to play.
With coconuts dropping, we summon our fate,
Now watch out for bees, they've opened a gate!

The vines twist and twirl in a merry ballet,
And ants wear tiny shoes, in a grand parade.
Laughter erupts as the sun starts to beam,
This world woven in green feels just like a dream.

So raise up your glasses, let's toast to the fun,
To the friends in the trees and the shines from the sun.
In this woven tale where the wild creatures prance,
Life's a silly giggle — just join in the dance!

Drawn to the Palm's Caress

Underneath the fronds, we discover delight,
With coconuts rolling like balls in a fight.
Palm leaves are fans, they swish and they sway,
While iguanas practice their best cabaret.

A breeze tugs our hats, what a raucous affair,
As crickets tap dance in this tropical lair.
With sunburned noses, we squint to the sky,
And giggle at clouds that float by on a high.

Laughter erupts from a cheeky old parrot,
Who claims he's a king but has no hidden merit.
We play hide and seek with the shade from the trees,
Ducking and diving — oh, can you believe these?

So here's to the palms that invite us to stay,
With their leafy embrace, they keep boredom at bay.
In this quirky haven, we come to confess,
Life's better with humor — in palm's sweet caress!

Breezes that Carry Forgotten Whispers

Whispers of sailors hang in the breeze,
As the wind tells secrets beneath waving trees.
Laughter and tales of adventures ahead,
As the seafoam giggles where conch shells are spread.

Coconut crabs wear their shells as capes,
While the seagulls steal fries — they're rogue little apes.
Every gust brings a chuckle, a giggle, a cheer,
In this land where the ocean meets sand full of beer.

Raindrops are playful, they jump in a dance,
Mixing with sunsets that swirl and entrance.
The sighing of palm fronds, a tune of delight,
Echoing softly through the deepening night.

So follow the breezes with eyes open wide,
For they carry the humor we all hold inside.
In this world where all laughter takes flight,
We discover each moment as pure, shining light!

Mythos of the Majestic Fronds

In the kingdom of palms, legends come alive,
Where the monkeys debate how high they can dive.
Each frond holds a story, oh, better than gold,
Of treasure maps drawn with wild tales retold.

Swaying and dancing, they orchestrate fun,
While the chipmunks hold court with jokes on the run.
The turtles wear glasses, perusing their books,
As they plot vacations with all of the crooks.

The great sloth writes letters — oh, what a slow post,
While the flamingos boast they can strut with the most.
They laugh at the sun's rays that tickle their toes,
In the realm of fronds where every jest glows.

So gather around for a show that won't end,
As the majestic fronds teach us how to pretend.
In this mythical world where laughter is king,
We dance to the tune that the palm leaves all sing!

Eternal Summer Beneath the Leaves

In a land of shade and laughter,
Palms sway like they're at a disco.
Sipping coconuts, we dance a rafter,
Cracking jokes that never grow old.

Sunshine tickles our tanned skin bright,
While lizards join in on the fun.
Flip-flops slapping, we'll party all night,
Who knew warmth could make puns run?

Napping in hammocks, we hold tight,
To dreams of beach balls and sun.
A seagull steals my fries—what a sight!
With him, laughter's never done.

Beneath the palm trees, time bends slow,
Witty comebacks float on the breeze.
As playful as a sea breeze in tow,
Here's to laughter—will you please!

The Allure of Endless Summers

Palm trees winking in the sun,
Coconut drinks in hand, oh fun!
Why did the chicken cross to the shore?
To chirp along with the beach's roar.

We chase the crabs who scuttle and dash,
They seem to know a good joke or two.
While the sun slips low with a golden splash,
We giggle at the seaweed's new tattoo.

With every hour, there's more to see,
Like a flip-flop lost on the sandy floor.
Let's dance with the tides and sing with glee,
In laughter's grip, we all want more.

Barefoot on the beach, we sway and sway,
As the sunset brings a fiery parade.
With humor in our hearts, we'll laugh all day,
In this endless summer, we won't fade.

Secrets Hidden in the Leafy Maze

Whispering palms hold secrets tight,
In shades where giggles find their home.
"A squirrel just stole my sandwich—what a fright!"
Under these leaves, I feel like a gnome.

Lost in a maze of leafy delight,
Where the shadows dance and the sun peeks.
What do you call a lazy kite?
A flying rug that's unique for weeks.

Racing the breeze, we twirl and spin,
While ghost crabs plot their midnight pranks.
Palm fronds swaying, a silent grin,
As if they wink at our old pranks.

In this garden where giggles arise,
Nature holds a comedy show.
With laughter wrapped in the palm trees' sighs,
Every moment here, a joyful glow.

Symphony of a Sunlit Haven

Under palm shadows, laughter rings,
As sunbeams flirt with the ocean's spray.
Why do seagulls prefer old flings?
Because their wings take the best buffet!

The breeze whistles notes of a happy tune,
While crabs strut their stuff in time.
If fish could dance, they'd join the swoon,
In this sunlit haven, everything's prime.

In flip-flops and shorts, we leap and prance,
A rogue wave tickles our toes.
Nature's stage sets a joyous romance,
As palm trees sway in do-si-do flows.

Each day unfolds as a playful chase,
Bright smiles stuck like sunscreen, we share.
With a wink and a bow, we embrace the space,
In this symphony, we show we care.

Dancing with Dappled Sunlight

In the grove, where shadows leap,
Lemonade dreams are far from cheap.
A squirrel cracks jokes at my chair,
While I try not to spill my fare.

Sunbeams giggle through the greens,
Tickling toes and acting keen.
I dance with light like it's a friend,
But trip on roots that never end.

A butterfly winks, looks so sly,
As it flutters, aiming high.
I'm just a mess of laughter here,
With sun-kissed cheeks and lemonade beer.

Oh, to revel in this bright jest,
With dappled sunlight at its best.
Every leaf is smartly dressed,
In laughter's arms, I'm truly blessed.

Where the Palms Greet the Sky

Tall hats of green wave from above,
Whispering secrets, calling love.
They sway and twirl like a dance hall,
While I attempt a graceful sprawl.

An owl hoots, giving me sass,
As I harbor dreams of class.
A raccoon snickers, peeking wide,
At my attempts to move with pride.

Wind tickles the air, it sings—
"Come join the fun; forget your wings!"
So I gallop, hop, spread out my arms,
Dancing like a fool, with its charms.

The palms overhead laugh with glee,
Planting giggles as they see me.
Together we sway, less shy tonight,
In a silly show of pure delight.

Serenity in the Canopy

Beneath the branches, dreams take flight,
With chirps and giggles, pure delight.
A sloth hangs low with wise old eyes,
Seems to laugh at all my sighs.

The breeze plays tricks, it pulls my hair,
While monkeys toss fruit without a care.
I dodge and weave, trying to stay,
As nature's pranks lead me astray.

Crickets audition for a show,
While I try to strike a pose down low.
With leafy laughter as my guest,
This canopy feels like a jest.

In this haven lush and bold,
Every moment a tale told.
I join the frolic, lost and free,
Wrapped in whimsy, just like me.

Swaying Sentinels of Dreams

Oh, sentinels of leafy grace,
You watch as I trip, fall on my face.
Grass stains and giggles fill the air,
While you gently shake, without care.

Your fronds wave like hands in cheer,
As I bumble along with raucous tear.
A parrot squawks, "What's the deal?"
And I just can't help but squeal.

In your shade, tales intertwine,
Where humor flows, and day shines fine.
I swear you're plotting mischief, too,
As I dance and twirl, lost in view.

So here we sway, all day long,
Under the sun, where we belong.
With chuckles, we brighten the scene,
In a world where everything's a dream.

The Language of Leaves and Winds

Whispers in the breeze, oh so clear,
Leaves chattering secrets, lend me your ear.
A palm tree winks, I swear it was true,
It said, "Why so serious? Have a drink too!"

Fronds flip-flap tales of sun and of shade,
While coconuts chuckle when dropped—what a trade!
The wind throws a party, with laughter galore,
Join in the fun, but don't stand by the shore!

Birds with sunglasses gliding so high,
Making a splash in the bright azure sky.
A leaf fell down, did a dance on the ground,
And all of us humans just laughed all around!

The night brings the stars—oh, what a sight!
As crickets crack jokes under the moonlight.
When palms start to sway, you better prepare,
For the laughter of nature, you'll find everywhere!

Fronds that Sing of Home

A symphony played by fronds in the sun,
They rustle and giggle, oh what fun!
With coconuts playing maracas, oh my!
"Shake it like you mean it!" they shout from on high.

Frogs on the lily-pads leap with such glee,
In a chorus of chaos, they sing merrily.
The breeze joins the tune, it's a jazzy affair,
While palm trees sway gently, without a care.

Sipping on smoothies made fresh from the trees,
While chasing away worries with whimsical ease.
The shade feels like home, where laughter's the theme,
In the land of the fronds, we're all part of the dream.

When night wraps its arms, and the stars come alive,
The crickets bring humor, they always provide.
In this playful retreat, where joy finds its way,
Fronds sing of a home, where we all want to stay!

Sunlit Shores of Endless Dreams

At sunlit shores, where the sea meets a grin,
Waves waltz and whirl, let the laughter begin.
Seagulls on surfboards, just look at them glide,
In this quirky paradise, joy can't be denied!

Crabs wearing hats, tip their claws to the crowd,
As shells hold a riddle, echoing loud.
While umbrellas do shimmy, they're dancing away,
"Join us!" they shout, "Come on, don't be gray!"

On sandy stages, we play our charades,
Where laughter's the rule, and sun never fades.
Each grain holds a story, a giggle, a wish,
In the tapestry woven of sunshine and swish!

Twilight brings sparkles that shimmer and sway,
With stars taking turns, in a cosmic cabaret.
In these sunlit shores, where dreams bloom and burst,
The joy of the moment is forever rehearsed!

Oasis of Solitude and Peace

In this quiet retreat, where silence can smile,
A cactus wears slippers, oh isn't that style?
The palms hold a conference, with whispers so soft,
While goats in the distance seem loftily aloof.

Water flows gently, it giggles and flips,
Each drop steals a dance, on invisible trips.
The rocks throw their back-to-back parties all night,
And invite every creature to join in the flight.

While hermit crabs bring their own brand of cheer,
In shells as their homes, they parade without fear.
"Why hurry?" they chant, "When you can just rest?
In this oasis, we're living our best!"

As moonlight descends, it sprinkles a glow,
On laughter so tender, and breezes that flow.
In this serene refuge, where quirks play and tease,
Peace isn't just silent; it also brings ease!

Sun-drenched Retreats of Serendipity

In a land where sunscreen's a must,
Sandcastles rise, but they often rust.
A crab steals my snacks without a care,
He winks at me, like a beach-time dare.

The flip-flops lie scattered, a game of fate,
While seagulls gossip and contemplate.
Ice cream drips, a colorful mess,
As I chase it down, I must confess.

Here laughter echoes like waves on the shore,
Sunburns reminding me to be careful, for sure.
A hammock sways, tempting me to nap,
But even that triggers a travel mishap.

In this sunny place where giggles collide,
Every moment feels like a roller coaster ride.
So raise a toast to fun and delight,
In sun-drenched retreats, it feels just right.

The Heartbeat of Tropical Life

Where coconuts drop with a thud at noon,
And a lizard dances to a calypso tune.
With every sip of my fruity drink,
A parrot squawks, causing me to blink.

Swaying palms whisper secrets to the breeze,
While monkeys swing with the greatest of ease.
A beach ball floats, it's quite the sight,
But crashes into me, what a funny fright!

Sunset paints the sky with laughter and glee,
As I trip on my towel, oh woe is me!
A pineapple grows an unintentional head,
Be careful, my drink might end up instead!

In this land where mischief comes alive,
The heartbeat of joy makes my spirits thrive.
With laughter as music, I dance through the night,
In this tropical realm, everything feels right.

Where Time Slows Beneath Skylines

Watches melt like ice cream cones,
Time moves slow, with silly tones.
A hammock hums, rocks to and fro,
Silly thoughts in the sun's warm glow.

The city skyline bows with grace,
While I attempt a sunburned embrace.
Laughter erupts as my hat takes flight,
Chasing it down feels like a comic night.

Cocktails adorned with tiny umbrellas,
Look like hats for thirsty fella's.
A surfboard's surfed, while you may slip,
Alternative sports with a laughable flip.

Where time stands still for a nonsensical act,
Each moment a comic, memorable fact.
So let your worries float high like a kite,
Underneath the slow skies, everything's light.

Clouds Embraced by Palm Shadows

In the shade where dreams take flight,
A cloud-shaped like a giant kite.
With palms swaying, throwing shade,
I lay here, in a giggle parade.

Barefoot, I stroll on a sandy quilt,
My drink spills over, oh dear, my guilt.
A turtle grins as I trip on my toes,
Under palm shadows, mischief just grows.

Dancing shadows play hide and seek,
While a cockatoo squawks, "Come take a peek!"
The sun beams down, wearing a smile,
As I hop like a frog, just for a while.

In this land where clouds hold hands with trees,
The laughter of nature floats gently with ease.
So join the fun, let your spirit dive,
In the blush of the day, we all come alive.

Lullabies of the Wind

Whispers through the leaves do sing,
Dancing like a silly spring.
The crabs wear sunglasses, oh so bright,
As they shuffle left and right.

Fronds sway in a wobbly way,
Tickling fish who come to play.
Turtles giggle as they poke,
At the starfish doing the yolk!

Coconuts chuckle on the ground,
Making friends with roots all around.
A seagull tried to steal a shoe,
But tripped on its own shadow, who knew?

Palm trees sway with sassy flair,
Throwing shade without a care.
They dance and twirl in breezy glee,
Who knew plants could be so cheeky?

Embrace of the Emerald Isles

Bubbles in the lagoon pop loud,
As ducks strut, oh so proud.
The sun wears shades, thinks it's cool,
While lizards lounge by the pool.

Mangoes juggling in mid-air,
Lime pies whisper, "Do we care?"
Bananas slip in a perfect line,
Saying, "We're on holiday, feeling fine!"

Dancing shadows on the sand,
Flip-flops hitch a ride, so grand.
Pineapples wear hats, look distinguished,
While crickets chirp, oh so mischievous!

The breeze tickles every nose,
As giggling waves do propose.
In this jest of nature's plan,
Laughter reigns in palm-tree land!

Secret Shores of Gentle Breezes

Seagulls wearing tiny hats,
Strut like little acrobats.
The sand is warm, it likes to tease,
While flip-flops play hide-and-seek with ease.

Crabs hold a party by the shore,
With seaweed snacks and a review galore.
"Who invited the octopus?" they say,
"Oh no, he's dancing—all day!"

Waves do the limbo, bending low,
While clams are singing a doo-wop show.
Impish dolphins jump and dive,
In this quirky beach, oh how they thrive!

Sunsets twirl in fiery gowns,
As night falls softly, brushing towns.
Stars winking down with a cheeky grin,
In the land where the laughter begins.

Echoes of a Palm-Lined Horizon

Breezes whistle a tune out loud,
As waves cheer on, feeling proud.
Palm trees gossip, swaying high,
While sunsplash giggles pass by.

Wiggling ants on a sandy spree,
Think they're in a seaside jubilee.
Coconuts rolling like bowling balls,
Challenging seashells in friendly brawls.

Starfish in sunglasses strike a pose,
While watermelons don't know where to go.
They all agree: nature's no bore,
Smile wide and dance on the shore!

As shadows stretch and the day grows old,
The laughter echoes, never cold.
In this jive of the palm-lined site,
Memories light up the starry night.

A Symphony of Pales and Light

In a sun-drenched space, the shadows play,
It's a dance of leaves, quite a grand ballet.
With each gentle breeze, they sway and twirl,
Like silly dancers in a merry whirl.

Bright fruit hangs low, with a cheeky grin,
Sipping on sunshine, a tropical sin.
A coconut falls—oh dear, what a splash!
It's party time, let's make a big dash!

Birds chirp their tunes, like a band on the run,
While lizards perform in the warm, golden sun.
A piña colada, just out of sight,
In this vivid play, everything feels right.

With palm fronds waving, a warm, funny cheer,
Come join the parade, let's all disappear.
Underneath the hues, where laughter stays,
Life's a joyous mess in so many ways.

Layers of Life Under Palm Canopies

Beneath the tall fronds, a rom-com unfolds,
Squirrels chasing tales that they've never told.
A rabbit trips over a bright, silly shoe,
Laughing with crickets, what a wild crew!

A parrot introspects on its colorful fate,
Mimicking giggles, isn't it great?
With fruit hat jokes and seaweed style,
Even a kid would crack a bright smile.

Bees debate buzzing, what's sweeter, who's best?
As flowers offer up their floral jest.
A turtle just waves, who's late for the show,
Taking his time, all laid back and slow.

Each layer is fun, like a cake full of cheer,
With flavors of laughter throughout the whole sphere.
Under the palms, where sweet stories drip,
Life's a delicious, hilarious trip.

Nature's Charm in Endless Green

In the lush emerald, a hammock swings wide,
With squirrels as acrobats, they take a wild ride.
A breeze whispers softly, tickling the leaves,
While the sun's warm embrace is what everyone believes.

A frog's ribbit echoes, a comedy night,
As bugs gather 'round for a laugh and a bite.
Tiny toes tap on the warm, sandy floor,
Who needs a dance club, when the outdoors can score?

Palm trees stand tall like bouncers at play,
Letting only the cheerful and funny to stay.
In the greenery's charm, life dances along,
Where each silly moment becomes a grand song.

Under the lush canopy, stories take shape,
With twists and with turns, no need for escape.
Nature invites with a wink and a grin,
Join in on the fun, let the laughter begin!

An Invitation to Tranquility

In a world wrapped in green, find solace on chairs,
A hammock awaits, with palm trees for pairs.
Oh fish in the pond, with your splash and your flip,
Make way for a giggle, let laughter be the trip!

With yoga mats spread, it's a quaint little class,
While ants do their yoga, they're quite the sass.
Birds glide on by, with sass on their wings,
Chasing clouds lightly, it's a dance that they bring.

Let's sip on some smoothies, filled with delight,
While a cat with a straw gets the order just right.
And soon we will find, in this silly retreat,
Every moment we cherish, is a fun little feat.

So come and relax, let the laughter unfold,
In the warm, happy palm, stories vibrant and bold.
An invitation to peace, but with a twist of cheer,
Join the merry band, for the joys of the year!

Fronds Behind the Curtain of Time

In the forest of shades, where the laughter grows,
The freckled sun dances, as the warm wind blows.
Palm hats on the heads of the giggling crew,
Making shadows that wiggle, just like the view.

Lizards wear sunglasses, looking quite chic,
Whispering the secrets, while the goats sneak a peek.
Coconuts chuckle, they bounce with delight,
As the stars play peekaboo in the velvety night.

Reflections by the Water's Edge

By the bank of the brook, where the ducks float in line,
Chasing their reflections, it's a waddle divine.
The frogs hold a concert with a quirky croak,
While the fishes jump in, for a splashy joke.

Sunbathed turtles spread tales of their speed,
While the dragonflies zoom in a shimmering deed.
Even the ripples giggle as they play,
Sharing each story of the bright, silly day.

Symphony of the Silken Breeze

A musical breeze tickles the leaves up high,
Palms wave like conductors, reaching for the sky.
The rustling laughter, in nature's own tune,
As butterflies dance beneath the bright moon.

Swaying to the rhythm of the soft summer light,
Mice on a picnic, nibbling bites with delight.
Comedians of nature, with jokes on a vine,
In this quirky orchestra, everything's fine.

Green Guardians of Forgotten Dreams

In the shade of the giants, where daydreams reside,
The whispers of past fables frolic with pride.
Squirrels in suits tell wise tales of yore,
While the shadows giggle at legends galore.

Mossy carpets giggle beneath tiny feet,
As ants march to rhythms, a whimsical beat.
Cacti in sunglasses serenade the night,
Guarding joy and laughter, a whimsical sight.

Dreams Etched in Tropical Gold

Beneath the sun, the monkeys play,
Stealing coconuts all day.
They cheer and hoot, with great delight,
While I just lounge, the world feels right.

The parrot squawks a funny tune,
Calling me a lazy loon.
I sip my drink, a little sway,
As palm trees dance, in bright ballet.

The sand crabs race, in flip-flop style,
Tripping over, with such a smile.
While I just chuckle, in my spot,
These tiny heroes give all they've got.

With every wave, I hear them laugh,
Their tiny feet, a wild giraffe.
In this land where silliness reigns,
I'm king of joy, while humor gains.

Island of Whispering Shadows

On this isle, the shadows tease,
Tickling toes, rustling leaves.
Mischievous breezes pull my hat,
I chase it down, how silly is that?

The iguanas wear sun hats wide,
Pretending they are on a ride.
With shades on eyes, they strut around,
In their coolness, laughter's found.

The breeze whispers jokes I can't recall,
As I trip over my beach ball.
Laughter echoes from palm to palm,
Like a sunbeam, oh so warm.

Their shadows dance, in patterns bold,
While I'm busy, feeling old.
But here I find, no room for frowns,
In this circus where fun abounds.

Whispers of Tropical Oasis

In a garden where coconuts grin,
Lizards compete, just to win.
They puff out chests, with all their might,
While I'm just here for a tasty bite.

The parrots gossip, so it seems,
About my never-ending dreams.
I take a sip from my bright cup,
As they squawk about a dress-up.

Waves crash the shores, a funny sight,
Seagulls stealing fries and taking flight.
I laugh aloud, join the show,
In this haven where smiles grow.

With every twirl of tropical breeze,
It's a festivity, not a tease.
Come join the fun, forget your woes,
In this giggle land, anything goes.

Shadows Beneath the Fronds

The shadows jiggle, the sun's a mess,
I trip on roots, oh what a stress!
While palm leaves whisper secret jokes,
I'm just here, among the folks.

Snapping turtles strike a pose,
Who knew they had such silly woes?
With every blink, they start to dance,
I join their funk, given the chance.

Bamboo sways, as if to tease,
The wind becomes my best of pleas.
I roll with laughter, what a ride,
In a tropical dream, no need to hide.

When evening falls, the stars ignite,
With jokes exchanged, it feels so right.
In every shadow, a comical friend,
This merry realm, with no end.

www.ingramcontent.com/pod-product-compliance
Lightning Source LLC
Chambersburg PA
CBHW050317100526
44585CB00016BA/1566